A
CHINES.

Grace

from

Whitstable

Mum

A Gift of
CHINESE COOKING

by Walter Long and Meili Lin

WEATHERHILL
New York • Tokyo

First edition, 1996

Published by Weatherhill, Inc., 568 Broadway, Suite 705, New York, New York, 10012.

© 1996 by Raymond Furse. Protected by copyright under the terms of the International Copyright Union; all rights reserved. Except for fair use in book reviews, no part of this book may be reproduced by any means without permission of the publisher. Printed in the U.S.A.

Library of Congress Cataloging-in-Publication Data

Long, Walter
    A gift of Chinese cooking / Walter Long and Meili Lin. — 1st ed.
      p.   cm.
   ISBN 0-8348-0377-1 (paper)
   1. Cookery, Chinese   I. Lin, Meili.   II. Title.
TX724.5.C5L67   1996
641.5951—dc20   96-31122
                                                          CIP

Contents

Preface	6
Ingredients and Cooking Tips	8

RECIPES

Cold Eggplant Salad	15
Shrimp and Pork Dumplings	16
Uncle Ba's Spicy Peanuts	18
Spinach and Meatball Soup	21
Fast Fish Soup	22
Soy Anise Chicken	24
Chicken With Red Peppers	26
Cinnamon Beef	28
Beef Shreds with Celery and Carrots	30
Quick-fried Lamb with Scallions	33
Fragrant Steamed Fish	36
Hot and Sour Fish and Beancurd	39
Spicy Shrimp with Water Chestnuts	40
Trout Steamed in Garlic and Black Bean Sauce	43
Pine-Nut Shrimp with Cucumber	44
Granny's Spicy Tofu	46
Braised Beancurd with Black Mushrooms	49
Asparagus with Crabmeat	50
Sichuan Eggplant	52
Garlic Bok Choi	54
Hot and Sour Cabbage	57
Tossed Sesame Noodles	58
Ants Climbing a Tree	61
Yangzhou Fried Rice	62

序 Preface

I never wanted to learn to cook Chinese food. I assumed it required an inordinate amount of preparation—lots of chopping and slicing of exotic ingredients that you could only find in a Chinatown grocery. Besides, why bother? Every American city and suburb has a Chinese restaurant, and most deliver. I didn't realize until I was served real Chinese food, during a year in Taiwan, that what I had been accustomed to eating was no more closely related to good Chinese food than is a MacDonald's hamburger to the real thing.

Still, I was reluctant to try cooking it myself until I lived in Japan, whose cultural heritage includes massive borrowings from the Chinese (supposedly "refined" to suit Japanese taste), as evidenced by a Chinese restaurant in every neighborhood. Unfortunately, these mostly serve Chinese food as uninspired and inauthentic as their American counterparts. Their most egregious culinary crime is serving bland *mapo doufu*, a Sichuan dish that is supposed to be hot and spicy. In Japan, and to be fair, in America also, it is too often sweet and insipid. Since this was my favorite dish, there was no recourse; I was forced to make it myself, and Meili showed me how easy it was to put together.

If you're new to Chinese cooking, try Granny's Spicy Tofu first (p. 46). It's simple: just stir-fry some chopped pork, garlic, and ginger and then throw in some beancurd chunks and hot bean paste. You'll have a spicy and healthful beancurd dish more delicious than you can get in ninety-nine percent of Chinese restaurants outside of China. Why? Because you made it the way the Chinese do, with no "refining" touches, and ate it hot and fresh without letting it gel into a blob in a take-out carton. All the recipes in this book are likewise authentic, simple, and delicious. In fact, they are delicious because they are authentic and simple, using only a few, fresh main ingredients.

Apologies are tendered in advance to anyone offended that this modest presentation makes light of a great culinary tradition. To master Chinese cooking is the work of a lifetime; even to choose dishes wisely requires a deep understanding of yin and yang, five-elements theory, and Chinese physiology. This is fascinating stuff, but you can't learn it all before the waiter comes for your order; likewise, you shouldn't let your ignorance of Chinese medicine and philosophy keep you out of the kitchen. The key is to go for variety in texture, flavor, color, and main ingredients. From the two dozen recipes selected here, choose one type of dish (meat, fish, vegetable) for each of from four to six diners and you'll have a feast that will be talked about for weeks to come.

Can you do it? When friends heard that we were working on this book they asked, "You're writing a cookbook?" in a tone precisely modulated to imply, "We didn't know you two could boil water." We're aware that this confession may not inspire confidence but the point is simply that we are not wizards with the wok; if we can do it, anyone can. And we guarantee that your family and friends, assuming they're not Chinese, will claim they have never had Chinese food as good.

NOTE: For those unfamiliar with the few American measurements used here, consider a pound to be about 450 grams, a cup to be about one-fourth of a liter, and an inch to be about 2.5 centimeters.

成份 Ingredients and Cooking Tips
==

All the recipes in this book are intended to serve four, assuming they are accompanied by rice and other dishes. However, since Chinese eating is "family style," with diners serving themselves from common platters, don't bother with the math required to figure out how to serve six; just add more dishes. The rule of thumb is one less dish than diners, e.g., five dishes for six people. If you are concerned about everyone eating their fill, do as the Chinese do: finish with a big platter of fried rice (p. 62). Although Chinese love sweets, meals are more often concluded with fruit and tea; thus no dessert recipes are included here. The ingredients required for Chinese cooking are today found on the shelves of most supermarkets. Before getting started, however, please read the following tips on ingredients and cooking methods.

OIL

Contrary to what many cookbooks assert, peanut oil is only rarely used in China; it is too costly. Likewise there is no need to purchase an expensive "wok oil" (usually cottonseed oil spiced up with garlic). Use whatever oil you prefer; the key to a rich and authentic flavor is freshly chopped ginger and garlic, the use of stock rather than water whenever cooking liquid is called for, and good rice wine.

STOCK

Bring a large stockpot full of water to a boil and then simmer for 2 to 3 hours: 2 pounds of chicken parts, 2 pounds of lean spareribs, a whole knob of garlic, 3 1-inch chunks of ginger, a few tablespoons of rice wine, a splash of soy sauce, one cut-up carrot, a sprig of parsley, three green onions, six stalks of dried mushrooms. Cook the meats and spices first, adding the vegetables in the last hour. Strain and chill the boiled mixture, and skim off the fat, which will congeal at the top, before using. Make a lot; you can freeze it for later use. Alternately, use the broth from the Soy Anise Chicken on p. 24. Note that this latter has a lot of soy sauce and wine in it, so add less of these ingredients when cooking with it.

VEGETARIAN STOCK

Stir-fry for 10 minutes in a few tablespoons of oil: a half dozen cloves of garlic, 6 1-inch chunks of ginger, and 2 pounds of soybean sprouts. Transfer to a stock pot filled with 2 quarts to a gallon of water, bring to a boil, adding a couple of peeled and sliced kohlrabi, a generous splash of rice wine, soy sauce, a cut-up carrot, a sprig of parsley, some green onions, and 6 stalks of dried mushrooms. Reduce heat, skim the froth, and simmer for 2 hours.

RICE

We prefer the longer-grained varieties, such as basmati or jasmine, because it seems easier to make fluffy, perfectly cooked rice with them. We have poorer luck with the shorter grained Japanese rice, which is stickier. Brown rice, of course, is richer in vitamins, minerals, and protein than the more polished white rices; however, it also has a stronger flavor, which some feel interferes with the taste of the foods served on it.

NOODLES

China has as many varieties of pasta as Italy, where, legend has it, Marco Polo introduced them upon returning from his travels in Cathay. Noodles made of rice flour and water are most common, although for stir-frying, egg noodles *(dan mian)* are preferable. Bean-thread noodles *(fen si)*, excellent in soups, are made from mung beans and are sometimes called cellophane noodles due to their translucent appearance. Most of the stir-fried recipes in this book would be equally tasty served on a bed of fried noodles rather than with rice. For this, use the very thin vermicelli noodles, also called rice-stick noodles *(mi fen)*, since they are made from rice powder and water. Heat a cup of oil in a wok, and drop in the vermicelli noodles (they are sold in blocks), fry for 6 seconds, turn over and fry an additional 6 seconds. Remove to a paper towel to drain. Break them up a bit and spread them out as a base for your stir-fried dish.

SOY SAUCE

Nowadays, even ordinary soy sauce comes in a bewildering variety, including "light," which refers more often to lower sodium content than to thickness. As soy sauce is the principal source of salt in most Chinese cookery, salt is often omitted as a separate ingredient in these recipes unless no soy sauce is called for. Add salt to taste.

BEANCURD

Called *doufu* in Chinese, and here referred to as tofu (now a respectable English word, from the Japanese pronunciation), this is available today in most supermarkets. The recipes in this book call for the firm variety rather than the soft, since it holds up better during stir-frying. Before cooking, press the water from the tofu pieces (typically 3 or 4 in a package) by arranging them on a plate and placing another plate on top, with some additional weight (a can of something) added. After 15 minutes, drain off the water that has been squeezed from the tofu. The tofu you don't use can be kept in the refrigerator for several days, but you must change the water daily.

BEAN PASTES AND SAUCES

A wide variety of these prepared sauces, with English labels, are now available in supermarkets; buy some and experiment with stir-frying any mix of tofu and vegetables. For the recipes here you will need hot bean paste *(douban jiang)*, sometimes called spicy bean paste. Anything labeled chili paste, a similar fiery red concoction but made with chili peppers rather than beans, is an acceptable substitute. Whenever black beans are called for, we prefer to use prepared black bean paste with garlic; then there's no need to mash beans or chop garlic. Finally, sweet bean paste, familiar to most of us as the sauce for Peking duck, will be appreciated by those who find the others too strong or strange. Its Cantonese version, called *hoisin* sauce, can also be used.

DRIED MUSHROOMS

These can be reconstituted by first rinsing and then soaking in warm water for a half hour or so. Trim off the woody, hard part of the stem before using and save the water for cooking or toss it into your stock pot.

CORIANDER

Some do not like the taste of this wonderfully fragrant herb, called *xiangcai* in Chinese. If called for as a garnish, parsley can be substituted.

SICHUAN PEPPERCORNS

Sold in cellophane bags, these whole reddish peppercorns have a unique flavor, and when used liberally impart a pleasant, spicy numbness to the lips. As with black peppercorns, a lesser but acceptable substitute, they should be stored sealed and ground fresh before using. For even more flavor, toast them a bit before grinding.

RICE WINE

Shaoxing wine *(Shaoxing jiu)* is the best rice wine for Chinese cooking, and it is worth going to an Oriental grocery to seek out. There is also a "cooking" version of this wine that is a quarter the price of the drinkable wine, but it is a little saltier and not nearly as much fun in the kitchen. Any rice wine, such as Japanese *sake,* is an acceptable substitute, and cooking sherry will do if a rice wine is not at hand.

CORNSTARCH

A tablespoon or so of cornstarch with twice as many tablespoons of water or broth is often used as a thickener, especially when ingredients are cooked in more liquid than they are served in. However, overuse of cornstarch thickener is responsible for much of the glutinous fare that bad Chinese restaurants deliver, so use it sparingly. In fact, you can drain off excess liquid in the finally stages of cooking and avoid using thickener altogether.

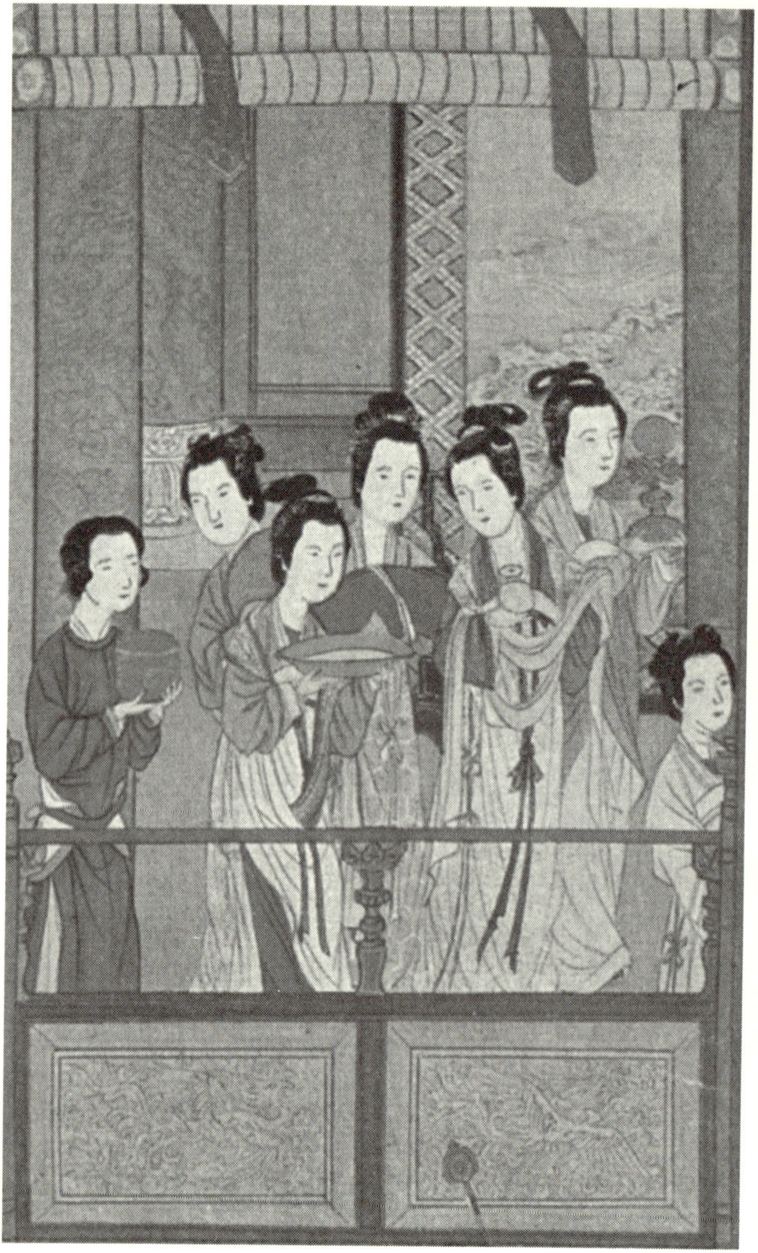

Recipes

In my opinion, chicken, pork, fish, and duck are the most delicious of foods, each having a rich and distinctive flavor; *bêche-de-mer* and bird's nest soup, as expensive as they are, in fact have no flavor at all.

—from *Shi Tan*, an eighteenth-century cookbook by Yuan Mei

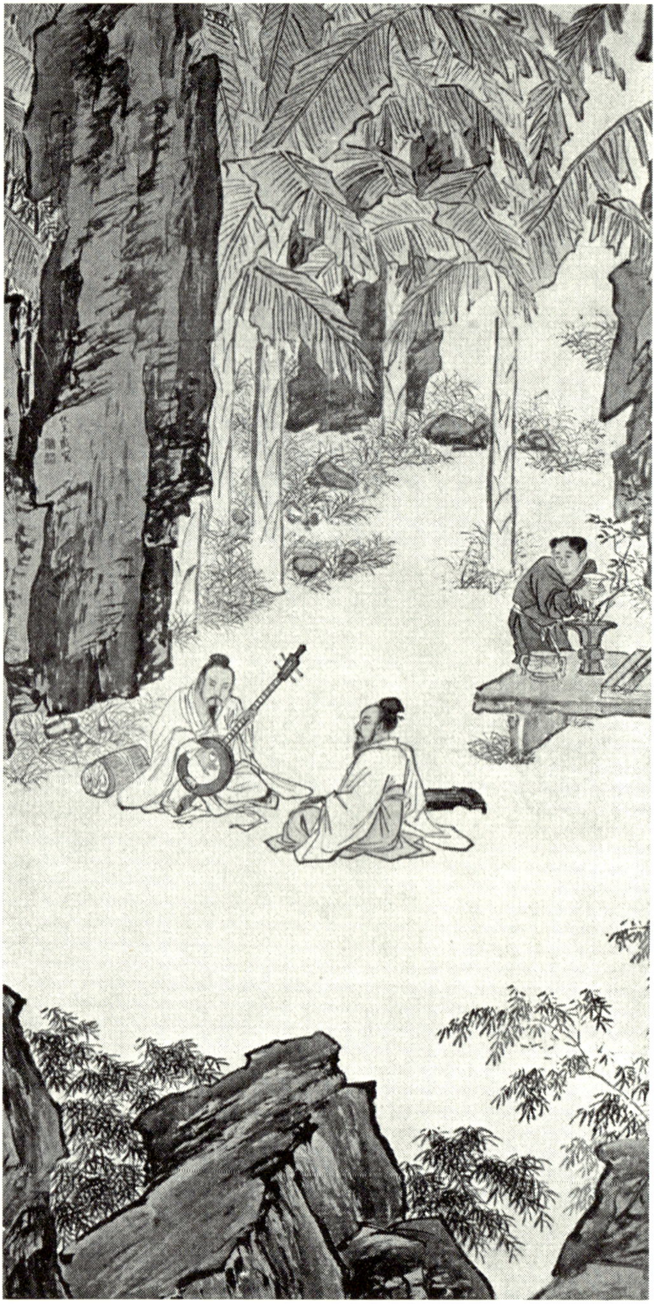

Cold Eggplant Salad
Liangban Qiezi

凉拌茄子

Eggplant is spongy and readily absorbs whatever flavors are around it, here sesame and coriander. For this reason it should be dressed just before serving. Adjust quantities of the dressing ingredients to taste, including the addition of salt, if desired.

INGREDIENTS

1	medium Western eggplant, or
3–4	small Asian eggplants
1 tbsp	toasted sesame seeds
1 cup	coriander leaves

DRESSING

2 tbsp	rice vinegar
1 tbsp	sugar
2 tbsp	soy sauce
2 tbsp	sesame oil

DIRECTIONS

Toast the sesame seeds in a dry frying pan over low heat for about 5 minutes. Set aside and let cool. Steam the eggplants for 20 minutes, until their flesh becomes soft and their skin wrinkled. If using a Western eggplant (rather than the thinner Asian variety) quarter before steaming and cut away center part that holds most of the seeds. Remove eggplant from the steamer, peel, slice lengthwise into strips about ½ inch thick, and drain on paper towels. In a separate bowl, mix the dressing ingredients. Remove the eggplant to a serving bowl and chill. Just before serving, stir and pour on the dressing, sprinkle on the sesame seeds and coriander, and toss very gently.

Shrimp and Pork Dumplings
Jiaozi

China has dozens of different dumplings and hundreds of dumpling recipes. Their amazing versatility makes them perfect party food: they can be cooked in advance and frozen, and then steamed, boiled, or fried for serving. Moreover, they can be stuffed with almost anything edible; at the risk of offending purists who insist that only pork and Chinese chives belong in this type of dumpling, the recipe below will assure that yours are memorable. The ingredients are actually those of a fancier dumpling dim sum lovers may know as *shao mai*. However, the folding technique is the simpler style of *jiaozi*.

INGREDIENTS

24	dumpling skins
½ lb	ground pork
¼ lb	raw shelled shrimp
½ cup	water chestnuts
1 tbsp	finely chopped garlic
1	eggwhite
1 tbsp	sesame oil
1 tbsp	finely chopped scallions
1 tbsp	soy sauce
1 tbsp	rice wine
¼ tbsp	ground black pepper
¼ tbsp	sugar

DIPPING SAUCE
soy sauce
rice vinegar
chili oil or sesame oil

DIRECTIONS
Devein, rinse, and mince the shrimp. Chop the water chestnuts into small bits. Combine all ingredients in a bowl and mix thoroughly. Chinese cookbooks sometimes include a recipe for

dumpling skins, although we side with those who think that homemade skins aren't worth the trouble (perhaps because ours are never as uniformly thin and delicate as the store-bought kind). Whichever you use, stuff a teaspoonful of the mixture into each skin, run a finger dipped in water around half the outer edge and fold over, pinching the edges to seal them. Here the real dumpling wizards get fancy, gathering and tucking to make a serrated edge, but any way you close them up they taste just as good.

Steam the dumplings in a steamer for 7 to 10 minutes, until the pork is thoroughly cooked. Although nested Chinese bamboo steamers look great when serving, an ordinary vegetable steaming rack, lightly oiled, works just as well. Instead of mixing the dipping sauce, put the ingredients on the table and let diners mix their own sauce in small condiment dishes; a standard mix would be half soy, half vinegar, and a dash of either chili or sesame oil. A teaspoonful of grated ginger will add zest. Leftover dumplings can be refrigerated or frozen for later use.

Uncle Ba's Spicy Peanuts
Boba Cuila Huasheng

伯
巴
脆
皮
辣
生

The Chinese have dozens of recipes for roasting peanuts, which are ubiquitous as appetizers and snacks with beer. The most colorful and delicious we have tasted were made with this recipe. The character for the name Ba is an old word for the region that is now Sichuan, probably where this recipe originated. Or maybe Uncle Ba is a real person. This dish can be made in a work as a stir-fry, but requires much less oil using this oven-baked method.

INGREDIENTS

2 lbs	salted peanuts (not dry roasted)
6 cloves	finely chopped garlic
2 tbsp	cooking oil
2 tbsp	chili powder
1 tbsp	coarse-grained salt
1 doz	small dried whole Sichuan chili peppers

DIRECTIONS

Pre-heat the oven to 325 degrees. Put the oil, garlic, and chili peppers in a shallow glass baking pan. Heat for 5 minutes, stirring occasionally. Add the peanuts and heat for 5 to 7 more minutes, stirring frequently. Remove, shake on the chili powder and salt (margarita salt or kosher salt work best) and toss thoroughly. These peanuts are great to eat right away, hot, but are even better after sealed and stored for a day.

插苗

岁朝清供
年来相尝案头笔一束
古人所必载有随物三色笺
也萧散古意
乙卯年岁除之 吴昌硕

Spinach and Meatball Soup

Bocai Rouwan Tang

We are always meeting Western lovers of Chinese food who are not impressed with Chinese soups, I suspect because they do not distinguish between the palate-refreshing clear broths (often simply the water from boiled vegetables or meat), and the more substantial course soups of the kind presented here.

INGREDIENTS

1 lb	ground beef, pork, and veal mixture, or meatloaf mix
10 oz	fresh spinach
6 cups	stock
3 oz	bean thread noodles
1 tbsp	soy sauce
1 tbsp	rice wine
1 tbsp	chopped scallions
1 tbsp	finely chopped ginger
½ tbsp	sesame oil
¼ tbsp	ground Sichuan peppercorns
½ tbsp	cornstarch

DIRECTIONS

Mix into the meat the soy sauce, ginger, rice wine, half the sesame oil, scallions, and cornstarch, and shape into small meatballs. Place the noodles in hot water for 10 minutes, then drain and set aside. In a large pot, bring the stock, pepper, and the remaining sesame oil to a boil. Add the meatballs, cook for about 8 minutes, then add the noodles and cook for another 4 minutes. Skim the froth, add the spinach, and cook for an additional minute. This dish is best served immediately, as the crisp and crunchy spinach contrasts nicely with the soft meatballs.

Fast Fish Soup
Yu Geng

With the fish chunks placed in the marinade and set aside, this soup can be prepared as quickly as you can boil water. We've recommended sole here, which simply melts in the mouth when prepared in this foolproof way, but any fish with comparably delicate flavor and texture will do. As a matter of fact, any fish at all will do; those who prefer more robust textures and flavors can substitute cod or even salmon (thoroughly cleaned of all skin and bones). And those who are not fans of coriander will probably be happy with Italian parsley.

INGREDIENTS

1 lb	fillet of sole or comparable fish
4 cups	stock
3 tbsp	chopped scallions
3 tbsp	shredded coriander leaves

MARINADE

¼ tbsp	salt
¼ tbsp	ground Sichuan peppercorns
1 tbsp	soy sauce
1 tbsp	rice wine
1 tbsp	finely chopped ginger
1	egg white
1 tbsp	cornstarch
1 tbsp	vegetable oil
½ tbsp	sesame oil

DIRECTIONS

Cut the fillet into 1-inch square slices; if the fillet is very thick, cut horizontally through the middle first so that the fish slices are not more than ½ inch thick. Mix the marinade ingredients thoroughly, then mix in the fish slices and set aside for a half hour or so. Heat the stock to a boil; add the fish slices, making sure they do not stick together. When the stock again comes to a boil, add the scallions and coriander, and additional salt and Sichuan pepper to taste. Remove from the heat and serve immediately, as the soft texture of the fish, just done to perfection, complements the crunchy bits of scallion.

Soy Anise Chicken
Jiangyou Ji

This has to be the world's greatest boiled chicken, with its soy and sugar glaze and traces of ginger, anise, sesame, and coriander. But it's just a boiled chicken—what could be simpler? Prepare it the night before and bring it out for an appetizer or party snack. The broth can be saved and frozen; it makes a great dipping sauce for plain boiled chicken.

INGREDIENTS

1	whole roasting chicken, 4 or 5 lbs
4–6 cups	water
2 cups	soy sauce
2 cups	rice wine
5 slices	peeled ginger, about 1/8-inch rounds
5	whole star anise
2 tbsp	sugar

DIPPING SAUCE

1/2 cup	finely chopped coriander leaves
1 tbsp	sesame oil
1/4 cup	broth from the boiled chicken

DIRECTIONS

Rinse the chicken and place two star anise and two rounds of ginger in the cavity. Put everything but the chicken and sugar in a stockpot and bring to a boil. Add the chicken to the boiling liquid. After 20 minutes, turn the chicken over, stir in the sugar and boil 20 more minutes. Baste portions of chicken sticking out of the liquid. Turn off the heat and let stand 2 hours. Remove from pot and let stand or refrigerate until serving. Retain several cups of the stock for the sauce; freeze the rest (it makes a great stock).

Slice and serve with a dipping sauce made up of the stock, sesame oil and chopped coriander to taste. For even stronger soy and sesame flavor, shred the meat and toss with the dipping sauce. For lower fat content, chill the broth and skim the fat before preparing the dipping sauce. The chicken can also be served over cold noodles of any kind and a pile of julienned cucumber to make a more substantial main dish.

辣椒子鸡 Chicken With Red Peppers
Lajiao Ziji

This dish was formerly called *zuo zongtang ji,* after a Qing-dynasty official named Zongtang, but since he was instrumental in suppressing some popular local rebellions, it is no longer politically correct in the PRC to honor him with the association. Too bad, for this elegant stir-fried chicken dish is tastier, prettier, and easier to prepare than its more popular Sichuan rival, chicken with peppers and cashews (*gongbao jiding*).

INGREDIENTS

1 lb	boneless chicken breasts
1	egg white
4 tbsp	cornstarch
4 tbsp	soy sauce
5	dried Sichuan peppers
2 tbsp	cooking oil
2 tbsp	chopped ginger
2 tbsp	chopped garlic
1 tbsp	rice wine
2 tbsp	sesame oil
2 tbsp	vinegar

DIRECTIONS

Cut the chicken breasts into ¾ inch or so cubes. Place in a marinade of egg white, half the cornstarch, and half the soy sauce for 15 minutes. Soak the red peppers to soften them, remove the seeds, and slice them into ¼-inch strips. Mix the rest of the cornstarch and soy sauce with the wine, vinegar, and sesame oil in a small bowl and set aside. Pour the excess marinade off the chicken.

Heat the cooking oil in a wok until very hot. Add the red pepper slivers, garlic, and ginger. Stir-fry for 20 seconds or so and add the chicken pieces. Stir-fry until the chicken turns completely white, about a minute, and add the bowl of seasonings. Thoroughly mix and cook 2 to 3 more minutes (until the chicken is done) and remove. This pretty dish, with its white chunks of chicken breast flecked with strips of bright red pepper, is delicious with rice.

> An old friend cooked up a chicken with millet,
> And invited me to his country home,
> Where green trees girdle the village,
> And blue hills rise beyond the walls.

—from *Visiting an Old Friend*, by Meng Haoran

挂
皮
牛
肉

Cinnamon Beef

Guipi Niurou

Guipi is literally the bark of the cassia tree, the Chinese cinnamon. It can be found in most Chinese groceries, but Western cinnamon sticks will also do. The chief delight of this dish is the fragrance and unusual taste of the fresh ginger mixed with cinnamon.

INGREDIENTS

1½ lbs	beef round, flank steak, or comparable cut
4 strips	dried or fresh orange peel, about 2 in long
¼ cup	dried Sichuan chili peppers
5 tbsp	cooking oil
2 tbsp	sesame oil
½ tbsp	rice vinegar
1 tbsp	crushed Sichuan peppercorns
1	whole star anise
1	cinnamon stick

MARINADE

3 tbsp	rice wine
½ tbsp	salt
2 rounds	ginger, about ⅛ in thick

GLAZING SAUCE

1 cup	water
3 tbsp	rice wine
1½ tbsp	soy sauce
1½ tbsp	sugar

DIRECTIONS

Remove fat from the steak and cut across the grain into ¼-inch strips. Toss in a bowl with the marinade and let stand from a few hours to overnight in the refrigerator. If you are using dried orange peels, soak them in hot water for 30 minutes. Remove the seeds from the dried chili peppers. Drain the beef from the marinade and remove the ginger. Heat 3 tablespoons of oil in a wok until very hot, and stir fry the beef, small portions at a time, until it is cooked through, adding more oil as needed. Remove with a slotted spoon and drain.

Wipe out the wok, reheat with a tablespoon of oil until very hot. Add the chili peppers, stir constantly until they turn black, then remove with slotted spoon and set aside. Add the Sichuan peppercorns, star anise, cinnamon stick, and orange peel, and stir fry for 15 seconds. Next add the glazing liquid and the beef and heat until boiling. Reduce to low heat, cover partially, and cook for 15 minutes or longer, stirring occasionally until sauce has been reduced to a glaze. Remove the cinnamon and star anise. Add the chili peppers, sesame oil, rice vinegar, and toss. Serve immediately with white rice.

Beef Shreds with Celery and Carrots

Ganbian Niurou Si

Some people are not fond of carrots and celery in a main dish, mentally categorizing these as salad fare. However, this famous Sichuan dish boasts hot and sweet flavors that can be balanced to taste, making a colorful and impressive dish for guests, as well as a budget-stretching way to serve beef to the family.

INGREDIENTS

1 lb	sirloin steak, or comparable cut
3 stalks	celery
3	carrots
3	fresh or dried red peppers
2	green onions
1 tbsp	chopped garlic
1 tbsp	chopped ginger
1–2 tbsp	hot bean paste
1–2 tbsp	sweet bean paste
1 tbsp	rice wine
½ tbsp	salt
½ tbsp	sugar
¼ tbsp	ground Sichuan peppercorns
1 tbsp	sesame oil

DIRECTIONS

Cut the beef, celery, and carrots into shreds: the beef should be cut first into slices across the grain then cut again into strips about ⅛ inch thick; the celery and carrots should be julienned as thinly as possible. Heat a few tablespoons of oil in the wok, stir fry the carrots and celery with about half the salt for a minute or so. Remove and drain.

Heat about 5 tablespoons of oil in the wok, add the beef shreds and stir-fry, stirring continually for about 8 minutes, until the beef is cooked to dryness. Add the bean pastes (hot and sweet according to taste), then the red pepper, the remaining salt, rice wine, garlic, and half the green onion, and cook for 3 minutes longer. Add the pre-cooked celery and carrots, stir fry for 2 more minutes, then add the Sichuan pepper, sesame oil, sugar, ginger, and remaining green onion for the last 30 seconds of stir-frying. Serve immediately with white rice.

32

Quick-fried Lamb with Scallions
Congbao Yangrou

Lamb is popular in northern and western China, where nomadic minorities have tended sheep down through the ages. This Shandong recipe calls for quick frying very thinly sliced lamb, and is the simple ancestor of the more complex mixtures cooked on a large griddle that we call "Mongolian barbecue."

INGREDIENTS

1 lb	lamb shank or comparable cut, thinly sliced
4	scallions
4	garlic cloves, thinly sliced
¼ cup	cooking oil
1 tbsp	sesame oil
1 tbsp	soy sauce
1 tbsp	vinegar

MARINADE

3 tbsp	rice wine
3 tbsp	soy sauce
3 tbsp	cooking oil
½ tbsp	ground Sichuan peppercorns

DIRECTIONS

Slice the lamb as thinly as possible, less than ⅛ inch is best; it is easiest to do this with frozen meat. Cut the scallions into 2-inch pieces, including most of the green ends, then cut lengthwise into thin shreds. Mix the marinade and toss in the lamb (you may need to let it thaw a bit); allow to stand for a half hour and drain excess marinade.

Heat the cooking oil in a wok until very hot and toss in the garlic slices. Stir-fry for 10 seconds and toss in the lamb, drained of excess marinade. Stir-fry until the lamb has almost completely turned from red to white, then add the scallions, sesame oil, soy sauce, and vinegar. Stir-fry briskly for another 30 seconds over high heat, remove, and serve immediately.

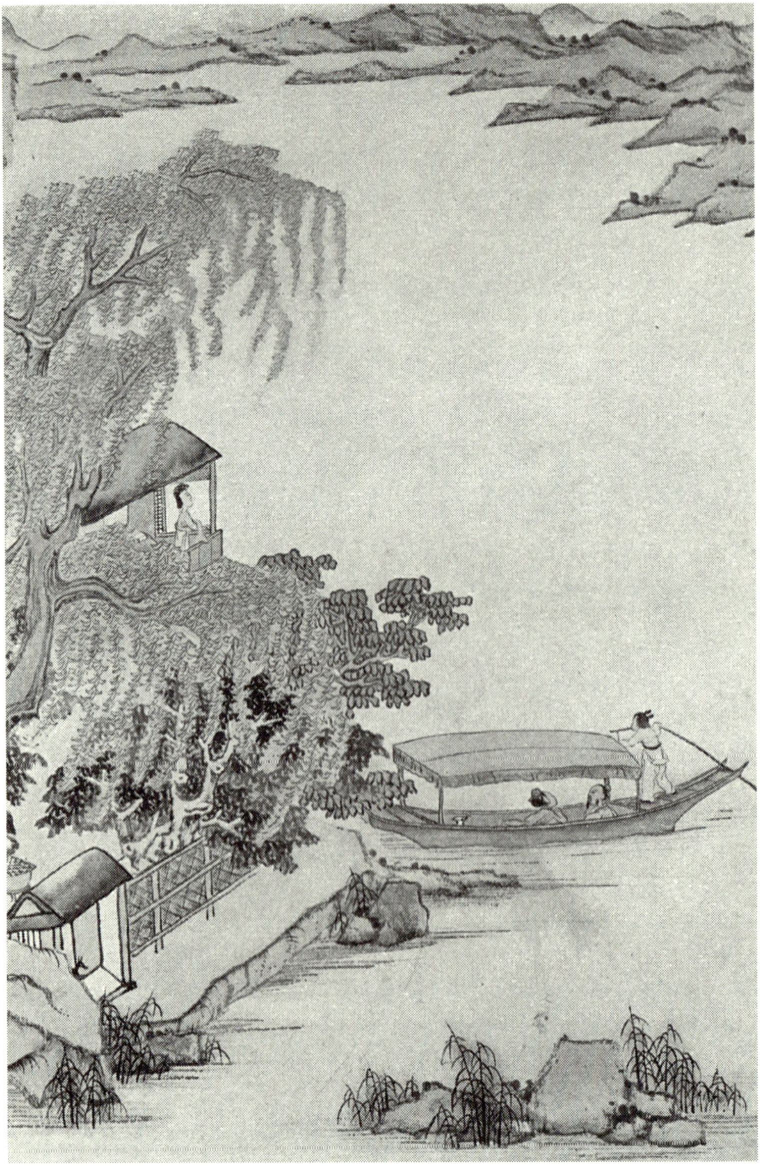

Mudfish are the lowliest of fish,
And really not appropriate for guests,
Moreover, being wiggly, slimy things,
They're quite a nuisance for the kitchen staff.
But Mr. Jiang was posted to the South,
Where his cook learned to make them perfectly.
His guest for dinner yesterday, I thought
They were the tastiest fish I'd ever had,
And learned as well: that lowly things can be,
Depending how they're seasoned, good or bad.

—*Mr. Jiang Serves Mudfish,* by Mei Yaochen

My wish is to be done with public life,
To take a bamboo pole and push off my boat
And make my home where fish and grain are plentiful.

—from *On the Occasion of the Bandits' Retreat,* by Yuan Jie

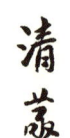

Fragrant Steamed Fish

Qingzheng Yu

The finer the fish, the simpler should be the method used to prepare it. If you find a perfectly fresh, whole fish with delicate white flesh (sea bass, grouper, baby turbot, etc.) have it gutted, scaled, and cleaned thoroughly, and cook it with this simplest of methods. Of course, the recipe works perfectly fine with any nice fillet as well. The object is to steam the fish so that it picks up obvious and flavorful traces of spring onion, ginger, and soy; adjust the quantities to suit your taste. Moreover, any fresh spices that you like with fish are suitable for this recipe; a favorite variation substitutes lemongrass and coriander, with no soy sauce (although, unlike the ginger and garlic, the lemongrass is not edible).

INGREDIENTS

1	fresh, whole fish, 2 lbs or better
10	spring onions
1	medium size chunk of fresh ginger
6 tbsp	light soy sauce
3 tbsp	chopped coriander leaves (optional)

DIRECTIONS

Trim and chop in half 8 of the spring onions; place these on the platter you will use for steaming. Wash and pat dry the fish and place it on the onions. Place several 1/8-inch slices of ginger (whole rounds) in the cavity of the fish. Cut the remaining 2 spring onions into 2-inch lengths and then finely chop lengthwise into the thinnest threads possible. Chop some of the remaining ginger into fine shreds in a quantity equal to that of the spring onions, mix all the shreds and sprinkle over the fish. Pour half the soy in the water for steaming, and steam for 10 to 15 minutes. When the fish is properly done you should be able to pull the flesh away from the backbone easily with a chopstick.

Remove the ginger slices from the cavity, pour the remaining soy sauce over the fish, garnish with the chopped coriander and serve. All the garnish is edible and delicious.

The cares of life are like a torrential flood;
I wish I could just be an old man with a fishing rod.

—from *Spring Boating on the Rouye*, by Zhi Wuchien.

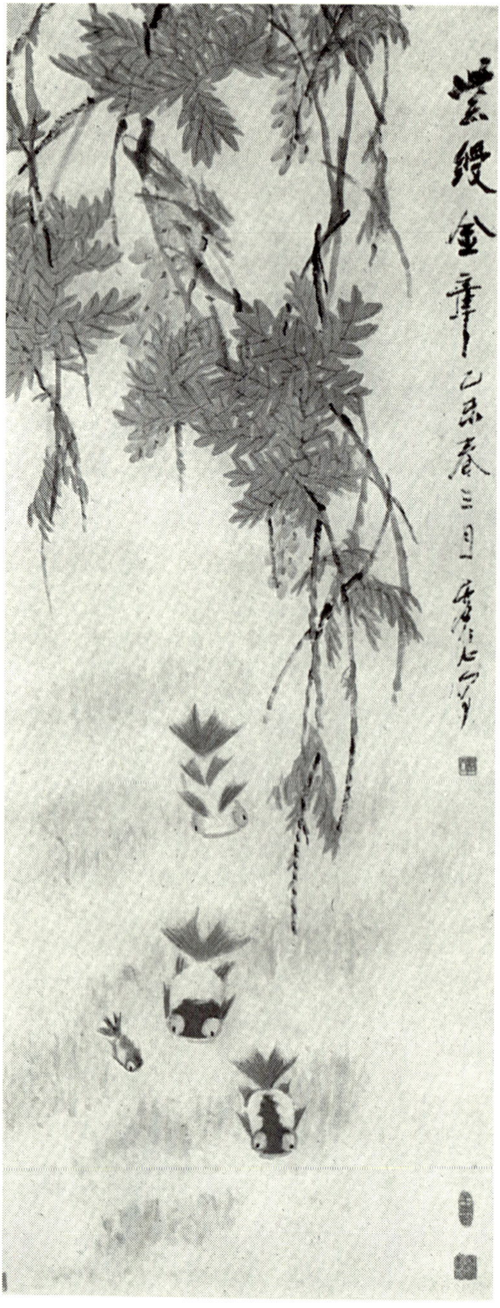

Hot and Sour Fish and Beancurd

Suanla Doufu Yu

酸辣豆腐魚

This easy dish is for those who love the wholesome no-fat, high-protein qualities of tofu, but find it unexciting without the addition of something extra, too often pork, which subverts these health benefits. The flavor of the fish—cod, halibut, snapper, or any fish that can hold together through gentle stir-frying—really comes through, enhanced by the spicy and sour combination of hot bean paste and wine vinegar, which can be adjusted to taste.

INGREDIENTS

2 squares	firm tofu
1 lb	fish fillets, cut into 1-inch cubes
3 tbsp	finely chopped scallions
1 tbsp	finely chopped garlic
2 tbsp	finely chopped ginger
½ cup	stock
3 tbsp	soy sauce
½ tbsp	sugar
2 tbsp	rice wine
1 tbsp	hot bean paste
3 tbsp	rice vinegar
¼ cup	chopped coriander leaves

DIRECTIONS

Marinate the fish cubes in a tablespoon of soy sauce. Drain and cube the tofu into similar-sized cubes. Heat a few tablespoons of oil in the wok, brown the fish, and remove. Heat another few tablespoons of oil, and stir-fry the garlic, ginger, and scallions. Add the fish and tofu, then the remaining ingredients except the coriander. Bring to a boil and simmer for 5 minutes (until the fish is done and the liquid cooked down a bit). Serve hot, garnished with the chopped coriander, with white rice.

Spicy Shrimp with Water Chestnuts

Lawei Xia

The bigger the shrimp the better for this flavorful Sichuan dish. The water chestnuts add a crunchy texture, but lightly steamed asparagus or broccoli can be substituted or added.

INGREDIENTS

1 lb	jumbo raw shrimp, shelled
6	dried, hot chili peppers
5 tbsp	cooking oil
2 cups	thinly sliced water chestnuts
2 tbsp	finely chopped scallions
2 tbsp	finely chopped ginger
1 tbsp	finely chopped garlic

MARINADE

3 slices	ginger, smashed
2 tbsp	rice wine
1 tsp	sesame oil
1 tsp	cornstarch
½ tsp	salt

SAUCE

¾ cup	stock
3 tbsp	soy sauce
3 tbsp	rice wine
½ tbsp	sesame oil
1 tbsp	rice vinegar
1½ tbsp	sugar
½ tbsp	cornstarch

DIRECTIONS

Clean and devein the shrimp, scoring the backs along the length (so that they will "butterfly" when heated). Place rinsed, drained shrimp in a bowl with marinade, toss and let stand for

20 minutes. Cut the dried pepper into $\frac{1}{4}$-inch sections, discarding the seeds. In a separate bowl mix all ingredients for the sauce. Heat a wok with $1\frac{1}{2}$ tablespoons of cooking oil until very hot. Remove the ginger from the shrimp and stir-fry half the shrimp at a time, cooking until they change color. Set the cooked shrimp aside. Wipe out the wok and reheat, adding 2 tablespoons of oil. Add the minced garlic, ginger, scallions and dried peppers and stir fry until the peppers turn black. Add the water chestnuts or vegetables and stir-fry for one more minute. Next add the sauce and cook until it thickens slightly. Add the cooked shrimp and toss. Serve with white rice.

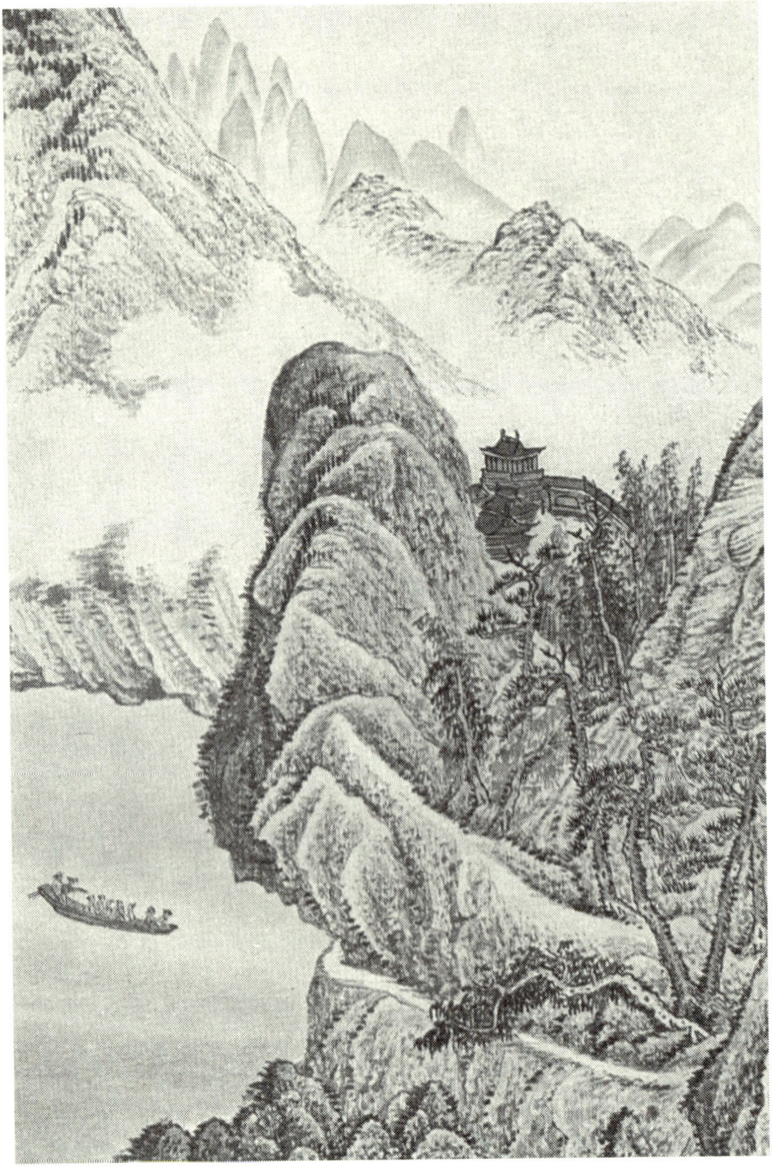

Trout Steamed in Garlic and Black Bean Sauce
Doushi Zhengyu

This is a favorite recipe for trout, but it works well with any other whole fish with delicate white flesh. Depending upon taste, other bean pastes, hot or sweet, may be substituted for the garlic and black bean paste. The secret of this dish is to apply the paste liberally to the skin of the fish, so that in steaming a subtle flavor is imparted to the flesh, but to remove the skin before serving, so that the flavor of the paste is not overpowering.

INGREDIENTS

2	trout or other whole fish, about 1½ lbs total
3 tbsp	black bean and garlic sauce
4 rounds	sliced ginger, about ⅛ inch thick
3 tbsp	chopped scallions
3 tbsp	cooking oil
2 tbsp	soy sauce

DIRECTIONS

Rinse the fish and pat dry. Place two rounds of ginger in the cavity of each fish. Spread the garlic and black bean sauce over the fish, and steam them in a wok or steamer for 8 to 10 minutes, until the flesh of the fish pulls easily away from the backbone, adding the chopped scallions for the last minute or so of steaming. Remove from the heat, scrape the black beans to the side, remove the ginger rounds, and pull the top layer of skin from the fish. Place on serving platter and spoon back on the black bean sauce and scallion mix to taste.

Pine-Nut Shrimp with Cucumber

Songzi Xiaren

Those who find the Spicy Shrimp with Water Chestnuts on page 40 too hot should enjoy this sweeter Shanghai dish. In fact, real shrimp lovers might enjoy them together, as they are complementary in color and flavor.

INGREDIENTS

1 lb	medium raw shrimp
3	small seedless cucumbers
3 tbsp	cooking oil
½ cup	toasted pine nuts
2 tbsp	finely chopped scallions
3 tbsp	finely chopped ginger
2 tbsp	rice wine
2 tbsp	sesame oil

SAUCE

2½ tbsp	stock
1½ tbsp	rice wine
1 tbsp	soy sauce
1 tbsp	sesame oil
¾ tbsp	sugar

DIRECTIONS

Toast the pine nuts in the oven at 350 degrees, until golden. Devein and score the shrimp along their backs so they will "butterfly" when heated. Rinse the shrimp, squeezing out as much water as possible using a paper towel, and toss in a marinade of the half the rice wine, half the sesame oil, and half the ginger. Let stand for 20 minutes or longer. Cut cucumber in half lengthwise, and the halves into quarters; then cut crosswise into one inch pieces.

Heat half the cooking oil in the wok and add the shrimp, drained of the marinade. Stir-fry about a minute, until the shrimp turn red, and remove to a paper towel to drain. Mix the sauce ingredients thoroughly. Wipe out the wok and reheat the remaining oil. Add the scallions and remaining ginger, stir-fry until the aroma rises, and add the cucumbers. Stir-fry about a minute, until hot throughout, then add the sauce and shrimp. Stir-fry another 3 minutes and add the pine nuts. Toss lightly and serve.

麻
婆
豆
腐

Granny's Spicy Tofu
Mapo Doufu

This Sichuan dish was supposedly invented by a woman named "Pocked-Marked Granny" *(ma po)* Chen; her "original" restaurant is still in business in the provincial capital of Chengdu. True or not, the dish is a favorite all over China. Unfortunately, it is too often toned down in Chinese restaurants in the West, with various ketchupy concoctions standing in for the all-important hot bean paste called *douban jiang* (see p. 10).

INGREDIENTS

1 package	firm tofu
2 tbsp	cooking oil
1 tbsp	chopped ginger
1 tbsp	chopped garlic
¼ lb	chopped pork
½ cup	stock
3 tbsp	rice wine
3 tbsp	soy sauce
3 tbsp	chopped scallions
3 tbsp	hot bean paste
1 tbsp	ground Sichuan peppercorns

DIRECTIONS

Drain excess water water from the tofu (see p. 10) and slice pieces gently into large (about ½ inch on a side) cubes. Heat the oil in a wok and add the garlic and ginger. Stir-fry a few minutes and add the stock, soy, and wine. When this mixture boils, add the tofu and half the scallions. Stir gently (so as not to break up the tofu chunks) and let simmer for a few minutes. Add the hot bean-paste, stir gently again, cover and let simmer another 5 minutes. Note that the heat of this dish comes mainly from the hot bean paste, so adjust accordingly.

Some cooks like to add a little cornstarch and water to thicken the mixture before serving, although we prefer simply to leave any excess liquid in the wok, ladling out the spicy tofu into a serving bowl and garnishing with the remaining scallions and Sichuan pepper to taste. This dish is always eaten over rice, so serve the rice in small bowls and have guests spoon on as much tofu as they like. Vegetarians note that this is a delicious dish even without the pork.

荷花開了
銀塘悄に
新涼早碧
翅蜻蜓多
通翁底艤
風曾那人
同里織手劉
蓮蓬記

Braised Beancurd with Black Mushrooms

Xianggu Pa Doufu

This is a dish for people who love Chinese black mushrooms, which for some reason have a richer flavor and denser, more pleasing texture after being dried and reconstituted than they do when fresh. The tofu, ostensibly the main ingredient, is really just along for the ride, carrying the rich flavor of the mushrooms and oyster sauce.

INGREDIENTS

3 squares	firm tofu
1 doz	dried Chinese black mushrooms
3–4	scallions, cut into 1-inch lengths
2 cups	stock
½ cup	mushroom liquid
3 tbsp	soy sauce
2 tbsp	oyster sauce
1 tbsp	rice wine
½ tbsp	sugar
2 tbsp	sesame oil

DIRECTIONS

Reconstitute the mushrooms and drain and squeeze the tofu (see pp. 10–11). Cut the tofu squares through the middle to halve their thickness, then cut diagonally to make triangles. Mix the stock, mushroom liquid, soy, sugar, wine, and oyster sauce in a small bowl and set aside. Heat a half cup of oil in the wok and fry the tofu, turning until golden brown. Remove and drain on paper towels. Remove all but a tablespoon or so of the oil and reheat the wok. Add the black mushrooms and scallions and stir fry for 30 seconds; then add the stock mixture and tofu, reduce the heat and cook for 10 minutes. Thicken as needed, and stir in the sesame oil. Serve hot, with white rice.

Asparagus with Crabmeat
Xiepa Lusun

Although not a traditional Chinese vegetable, asparagus, like many other greens, is delicious simply steamed in a bit of oil, stock, ginger, and rice wine. The addition of crabmeat, however, elevates an ordinary dish to an elegant one, and brings out the natural sweetness of the asparagus.

INGREDIENTS

1 lb	asparagus
6 oz	cooked crabmeat
6 tbsp	cooking oil
½ cup	stock
2 tbsp	finely chopped ginger
4 tbsp	rice wine
1 tbsp	finely chopped garlic
4 tbsp	finely chopped scallions

SAUCE

1 tbsp	oyster sauce
4 tbsp	stock
½ tbsp	cornstarch

DIRECTIONS

Wash and trim the asparagus, and cut on the diagonal into 2- to 3-inch pieces. Heat half the oil in a wok. Add half the ginger and let it sizzle, then add the asparagus and toss to mix. Add half the rice wine and half the stock. Bring to a boil, cover, and simmer for a few minutes—depending upon how thick the asparagus is and how crisp you like it—and remove with a slotted spoon.

Mix the sauce ingredients thoroughly and set aside. Clean the wok and reheat the remaining oil. Add the garlic, the remaining ginger, and the scallions. Stir-fry until the aroma rises and then add the crabmeat and the remaining rice wine.

When the crabmeat is hot throughout, add the sauce and stir-fry till the mixture thickens. Pour over the asparagus and serve immediately with white rice.

Sichuan Eggplant
Yuxiang Qiezi

My theory for why this stunning eggplant dish is not on restaurant menus everywhere is that its name is too often translated literally, as "fish-fragrant eggplant." *Yuxiang* is actually a Sichuan cooking style that calls for stir frying in garlic and hot bean sauce; there is no fish in it. This dish is beautiful, with the heat-brightened purple eggplant skins flecked with red pepper and green scallion bits, and is just as impressively delicious. If you have an Asian grocery nearby, buy Asian eggplants (smaller and skinnier than their Western cousins). If you use a Western eggplant, cut out a chunk of the seedy center so that each piece you cook has both skin and flesh.

INGREDIENTS

1	large, round Western eggplant or
4–5	small Asian eggplants
¼ cup	cooking oil
½ cup	stock
5 tbsp	chopped garlic
2 tbsp	chopped ginger
5 tbsp	chopped scallions, with the white and green separated
3 tbsp	hot bean paste
1 tbsp	rice wine
2 tbsp	sesame oil
2 tbsp	rice vinegar
4 tbsp	soy sauce
½ tbsp	sugar

DIRECTIONS

Slice the eggplant in 1½-inch to 2-inch strips, so that none are thicker than ¾ of an inch, with as many chunks as possible retaining the skin. Stir-fry in a "larger half" of the cooking oil. The eggplant will quickly absorb the oil, but keep up the heat until you feel the eggplant might burn. Then add a half cup of water or chicken stock and cover for a minute or so. When the eggplant steams to softness, remove and drain on paper towels.

Heat the remaining oil until very hot. Add the garlic, ginger, white scallions, and, after a few seconds, the hot bean paste, rice wine, sesame oil, vinegar, soy, and eggplant. Stir-fry until the eggplant is tender; if there is excess liquid, pour off or add a bit of the cornstarch and water. Remove to a serving dish and add the green portion of the chopped scallions for garnish. This dish is supposed to be served hot, over white rice, but since the eggplant absorbs the flavors so well, it's also great cold or reheated.

Garlic Bok Choi

Suanzi Baicai

This is one of many recipes that demonstrate how simple stir-frying can enhance the flavor, color, and texture of fresh vegetables. Those who are impressed with these benefits should experiment with different vegetables, spices, and seasonings. To get you started, variations for green beans and spinach are given below. Bamboo shoots (half a small can, drained) add variety, crunch, and contrasting color to any of these recipes.

INGREDIENTS

1 lb	bok choi
4 tbsp	cooking oil
2 tbsp	finely chopped garlic
½ tbsp	salt

DIRECTIONS

The basic steps for stir-frying are the same for all vegetables:
1) wash, trim, and slice vegetables into pieces of appropriate size;
2) stir-fry in oil and spices, thicker pieces first and longest, until nearly done;
3) add additional seasonings as needed;
4) remove and serve immediately.

For this recipe, wash and trim the bok choi leaves and stems, and cut crosswise in 2-inch strips. Separate into thick and thin parts, so that the thicker can be started first and thus cook longer. Heat the oil in a wok, add the garlic when the oil is hot, stir, and add the thicker pile of bok choi pieces. Stir-fry for 1 minute, add the salt and remaining bok choi, and stir-fry for another 2 minutes, until the leaves are wilted, but the stems still crisp. Variations:

SESAME SPINACH

Stir-fry for 1 minute in oil, then add a seasoning mix made up of 1 tbsp rice wine, 1 tbsp soy sauce, ½ tbsp rice vinegar, 1 tbsp sugar, and ½ tbsp salt. Stir-fry another minute, add ½ tbsp of sesame oil, and serve.

SWEET GINGER BEANS

Stir-fry for 1 minute in oil and 1 tbsp of grated ginger and 2 tbsp of chopped scallions. Then add a seasoning mix made up of ½ tbsp brown sugar and ½ tbsp soy sauce mixed in ¼ cup of stock. Reduce heat and cook 5 to 6 minutes, until beans are tender, and serve.

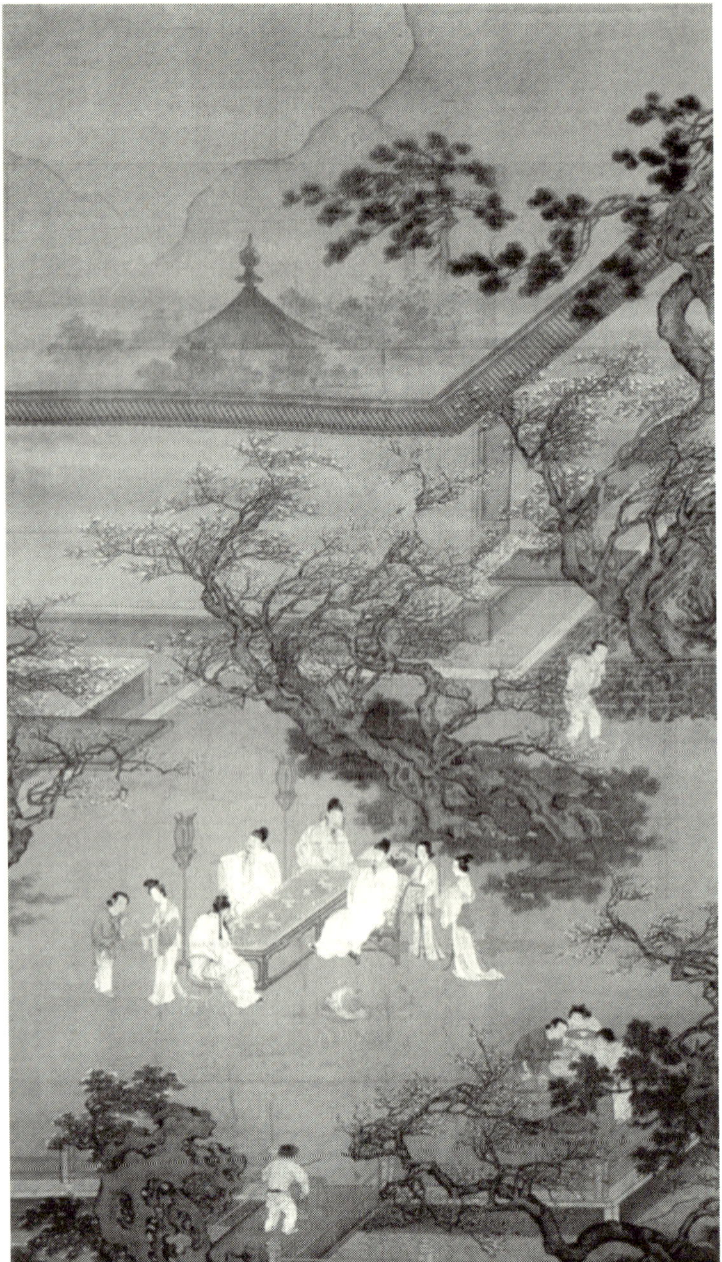

Hot and Sour Cabbage

Suanla Baicai

This wonderful cabbage dish from northern China is a perfect example of how an imaginative combination of spices can perk up a very ordinary vegetable. There are several varieties of Chinese cabbage; the most commonly available in Western supermarkets is called Napa cabbage.

INGREDIENTS

2 lbs	Chinese cabbage
3 tbsp	cooking oil
1 tbsp	rice wine
1 tbsp	sesame oil
6	dried chili peppers, seeded and chopped
1 tbsp	ground Sichuan peppercorns
2 tbsp	finely chopped ginger
1 tbsp	soy sauce
1 tbsp	rice wine
1 tbsp	rice vinegar
1 tbsp	sugar
½ tbsp	cornstarch
½ tbsp	salt

DIRECTIONS

Trim cabbage stem and discard wilted outer leaves. Wash and cut remaining leaves into 2-inch strips. Heat the oil in a wok and stir-fry the thicker half of the cabbage pieces over high heat for about a minute. Add the rest of the cabbage and stir-fry for another 30 seconds. Remove the cabbage and set aside.

Reheat the wok, adding the sesame oil. When very hot, add the dried chili peppers, Sichuan peppercorns, and ginger, and stir-fry for a few seconds, until fragrant. Add the cooked cabbage and stir-fry for 30 more seconds. Add the soy sauce, rice wine, vinegar, sugar, cornstarch, and salt. Toss gently cooking until the sauce slightly thickens. Transfer to a plate and serve with white rice.

凉
拌
麵

Tossed Sesame Noodles
Liangban Mian

This is one favorite selected from innumerable cold noodle dishes tossed with a sauce and garnishes, China's pasta salads. This variation calls for a sweet sesame sauce (which makes a good salad dressing by the way) with shrimp and chicken; another favorite sauce is coriander sesame sauce (p. 24). Optional garnishes are celery, scallions, thin slices of ham, pork, or omelet.

INGREDIENTS

½ lb	egg noodles
1 cup	shredded white chicken meat
½ lb	cold, peeled shrimp
½ cup	thinly sliced black mushrooms
1 cup	bean sprouts
1 cup	peeled and julienned cucumber
1 cup	peeled and julienned carrots
1 cup	shredded lettuce
¼ cup	chopped coriander leaves

SAUCE

6 tbsp	soy sauce
3 tbsp	rice vinegar
2 tbsp	rice wine
2 tbsp	sesame oil
1 tbsp	sugar
½ tbsp	salt

DIRECTIONS

Bring water to a boil and toss in the noodles for 2 to 3 minutes. Drain and rinse them with cold water and set aside. For the chicken, shred the leftover meat from your soup stock, the Soy Anise Chicken (p. 24), or any plain boiled piece. Fresh shrimps sauteed in a little chopped garlic and oil are best, but let the supermarket do the work if you choose. Reconstitute the dried mushrooms and slice all the vegetables. The crunchier the vegetable the thinner it should be sliced: $1/8$ of an inch is fine for the mushrooms, cucumber, and lettuce, as thin as possible for the carrots. Mix the sauce ingredients thoroughly and set aside.

Fluff the noodles, place them in a large bowl, and arrange the garnishes in bunches around the top. The shrimp and coriander are typically piled in the center, with the long thin strips of the other garnishes radiating outward, but any nice-looking arrangement will do. At the table, pour on the sauce and toss, thoroughly mixing all ingredients. Serve in small bowls, with a dab of chili paste or Chinese mustard on the side. This can also be served as a individual main dish. Split the ingredients, arrange them in small bowls, and let guests toss their own. This is a very refreshing summer dish when served chilled.

賓客坐位
卓子排設

Ants Climbing a Tree
Mayi Shangshu

螞蟻上樹

By way of explaining the odd name of this dish, it is asserted that the finely chopped pork and vegetables remind Chinese of ants. We can accept that, but how do noodles resemble a tree? Note that tidbits of almost anything you like can assume the role of "ants"—even chopped carrots or celery—and the pork can be omitted with absolutely no loss in flavor.

INGREDIENTS

3 oz	cellophane noodles (bean thread noodles)
¼ lb	ground pork
3–4 tbsp	finely chopped water chestnuts
3–4 tbsp	finely chopped black mushrooms
2–3 tbsp	finely chopped scallions
2–3 tbsp	finely chopped garlic
2 tbsp	finely chopped ginger
2 tbsp	cooking oil
1 tbsp	soy sauce
1 tbsp	rice wine
2 tbsp	hot bean paste
1 cup	stock
¼ cup	parsley or coriander, chopped

DIRECTIONS

Soften the cellophane noodles by pouring hot water into them. Let them stand for 10 minutes, then drain. While waiting, chop finely all the vegetables to make the "ants." Heat the oil in the wok and add the garlic, ginger, water chestnuts, mushrooms, scallions, and pork. Stir-fry for 3 minutes, then add the hot bean paste and stock. Continue to stir fry and add the noodles. Cover and simmer until the liquid has nearly evaporated. Following through with the "ants invading your picnic" theme, serve with a green garnish, chopped parsley or coriander.

Yangzhou Fried Rice
Yangzhou Chaufan

There are actually people who claim to dislike fried rice, because they've only had the fare served up by cheap take-outs, typically a sodden brick drowning in oil and soy sauce. Good fried rice is a fluffy and delicious one-dish meal, replete with the distinctive and distinguishable tastes of whatever ingredients you care to toss in; the Chinese like to use up last night's leftovers. For the best results, use rice that is a day old. I also believe that a modest amount of pork really makes the dish. Best is the red-cooked pork that Cantonese call *char siu*; otherwise, leftover meat from spareribs, pork tenderloin, or even ham will do. This recipe calls for shrimp, but chicken, shredded or chunks, will work just as well. What's in the fridge?

INGREDIENTS

1	egg
4 cups	cooked rice, at least a day old
¼ cup	cooking oil
1 cup	peeled shrimp of any size
¼ cup	chopped ham, pork, or Chinese barbecued pork
1–2	finely chopped scallions
3–4	finely chopped garlic
2 tbsp	finely chopped ginger
½ cup	frozen peas, thawed
1 tbsp	soy sauce
2 tbsp	rice wine
1	lime, quartered (optional)
1	cucumber, trimmed and sliced as desired (optional)

DIRECTIONS

Whip the egg and cook it separately, heating a tablespoon of oil in the wok, pouring in the egg, and swirling it around until it makes a thin pancake. Remove and slice into thin strips.

Heat the remaining oil and add the ginger, garlic, and scallions. Stir-fry for a minute and add the pork (assuming it is cooked, a leftover), the shrimp, and the peas. After one minute add the cold rice. It will probably stick together in a block; dribble the rice wine and soy sauce over it, and it will "steam" down into submission. Stir-fry vigorously for 5 minutes (the more you turn over the rice to keep it from sticking, the less oil you have to use), then add the egg. Stir-fry another minute. Although this is a Chinese cookbook, nobody serves fried rice as delicious as the Thais do, with slices of cucumber and lime; lime drizzled over fried rice transforms the mundane into the ethereal.

Mothers and daughters bring baskets of food,
Children and toddlers haul porridge in pots,
A line of them bringing food to the field hands,
Toiling on the southern knoll.

—from *Watching the Reapers*, by Bo Zhuyi

The children prepare a feast for me: wine,
Spring leeks gathered in the night rain,
And millet sprinkled over steamed rice.

—from *For Retired Scholar Wei*, by Tu Fu

The "weathermark" identifies this book as a production of Weatherhill, Inc., publishers of fine books on Asia and the Pacific. Book and cover design: Mariana Canelo. Production supervision: Bill Rose. Printing and binding: Daamen, Inc. The typeface used is Baskerville.